surprised by serenity

Acknowledgments

This book grew out of workshops given by Randy at a number of companies, including New York Life, Prudential, Mannatech, Lee Hecht Harrison, and others. We sincerely thank those who embraced these ideas and encouraged us to transform them into the printed word.

It is our strong desire that this book spark a dialogue with those interested in making a change in their lives and the lives of others. To this end, we would love to hear from you at our email address: randy.zack@worldnet.att.net .

Finally, we acknowledge those without whom this book would never have come to fruition: Kathy Marshall, Becky Miller, Sissy Massad, and Mary Anna Kidd.

Table of Contents

Wired for Wonder:
A New Look at the Serenity Prayer

He wakes up in the middle of night with a gnawing sense of anxiety. A problem from work worms its way into his consciousness, and it won't let go. He thinks of all the options, and the night ebbs on. He turns and regards his wife in slumber. She is his lovely partner of twenty years, and her slow, relaxed breathing pattern reminds him of how much he loves her and loves caring for her. Yet he recalls a harsh word after dinner and wonders if they have lost their passion for each other. He thinks about their early years and the magical times they shared. Where is that magic now? He wants it back and is willing to work hard to retrieve it, but the dread returns. How in the world will he ever find his way back to that romantic feeling? From the other side of the house he hears his teenage daughter coughing. Her asthma is flaring up again, and the medicine does not seem to quell the incessant cough. He wonders if perhaps she is allergic to something in the house.

And now the night seems to fold in upon itself, and he feels something beyond anxiety. A severe sense of loneliness and futility. He has no idea how he has arrived at this dreary place, and he turns to shake free of these doldrums. In the wee small hours, he finally manages to catch a few moments of sleep.

When he awakes in the morning, he feels better. As the first one up, he likes to get the household going. The mere smell of the coffee is enough to renew his sense of optimism and purpose. His wife and daughter greet him with sleepy smiles as he prepares breakfast. The uneasiness of the previous night seems to fade in the dawning day. He opens his daytimer to review his morning schedule, and suddenly he is struck numb again when he sees the name of the person who has been causing him problems at work. They are scheduled to meet, and as he considers the various strategies to resolve the problem, he begins to sense the same anxiety from last night. His wife and daughter are discussing an article in the paper. They turn to include him in the discussion, but he is already a thousand miles away.

Who is this man? He is you and me. He is Everyman. Why is he so troubled? He has a nice home, a little extra money in the bank, and a decent job. He loves his family and takes good care of them. Yet something is missing. He has no abiding sense of peace and well-being. Small problems nip at his heels and a growing sense of anxiety festers in him. When he takes stock of his situation, he believes that people and processes and forces beyond his control frustrate him and leave him feeling helpless at times. And it is this helplessness that is at the source of his anxiety.

If any of this sounds familiar, then I invite you to keep your mind and heart open to the suggestions and strategies offered in this book. While no one is immune to the cycles of anguish and pain that accompany all of us in our journey through life, we are able to change how we allow outside circumstances to affect us. And this change is not so mysterious as we often try to make it.

Getting Stuck
The Problem

Fear is a core emotion that has a strong grip on all of us.

It comes in three flavors. The first is fear of the future. We look for guarantees, but there aren't many out there. Sickness and death are inevitable. Beyond that, uncertainty looms like a gathering storm.

The second fear is anxiety of the present.. Have you ever noticed how "daily" life is? Like the salmon fighting their way upstream to spawn, we gather our bumps and bruises with each passing day. I call it "the Glory of the Grind." The older we get, the more we know that life is both joy and ruin. It has a wondrous, bittersweet quality. That's just under the surface. We ask ourselves, "When's this going to end? I'm bumping up near heaven now, but when's the trap door going to come?"

The third fear that lurks nearby is guilt from the past. Let's face it. We all have a few skeletons in the closet. We should have done something we didn't do. We held back, and now we feel that nagging sense of guilt. We opened our mouths and out came corrosive words that can never be retrieved. We all bear these burdens of the heart which we struggle to shed.

Is it realistic to think of strategies to diminish these fears? The answer is as simple and direct as a few words scribbled on a piece of scrap paper 50 years ago. After delivering a closing prayer at his church service, Reinhold Niebuhr was asked by a friend to transcribe these humble words, which have since become more famously know as the Serenity Prayer.

"God grant me the serenity
To accept the things I cannot change,
The courage to change the things I can,
And the wisdom to know the difference.
Living one day at a time;
Enjoying one moment at a time;
Accepting hardship as the pathway to peace.
Taking, as He did, this sinful world as it is
Not as I would have it.
Trusting that He will make all things right
If I surrender to His will.
That I may be reasonably happy in this life,
And supremely happy with Him forever in the next."

Niebuhr focuses on the number one principle for mental, emotional, and spiritual health: to know the difference between goals and desires. We are continually frustrated in our professional and personal lives because we have misunderstood the two terms. Our culture indiscriminately throws the term "goal" around like everybody knows what it means. Sales teams talk about setting goals, athletic teams have goals for reaching the playoffs, and distraught parents make it a goal to get their "prodigal" son or daughter to walk the straight and narrow.

If you were asked the question, "Do you think it's a good goal to have a happy marriage?" how would you respond? Or try this one: "Is it a good goal to raise terrific kids?" Most of us would answer a resounding "Yes!" My contention is that the answer is a decided "No," and it's because we have not clearly understood the word "goal."

The underlying issue in knowing the difference between goals and desires is to understand <u>who</u> <u>is</u> <u>in</u> <u>control</u>. **A goal** is that which you alone can accomplish. It is dependent on no one or nothing else. It is completely within your control.

A desire is that which is dependent on someone else or something else. It is out of your control.

Peeling Back the Layers

Let's begin our exploration of goals versus desires by looking at it through two circles that represent a life. Call these "Circles of Control."

The inside circle labeled **responsibility** represents those areas in our direct control. The outside circle labeled **concerns** represents those areas of life outside our direct control. Which circle at any given point in time is bigger? It's always the circle of concerns. Much more – from our skin color, the weather, other people – is out of our control.

We are responsible for those areas under "responsibility." The cliche, "If it is to be, it is up to me," falls in this category. If it's going to get done, I've got to do it. But a key question emerges: if we focus on the inside circle, what happens? It gets bigger. What gets smaller? Almost magically, the outer circle of concerns is reduced. The opposite is also true. By concentrating on the outer circle, it gets bigger and dwarfs the inside circle. One might call this the "Glance-Gaze" principle. We are to gaze at the center circle, focus and glance at the concerns (to not do so is avoidance or denial). But we are to never flip the focus. To do so is to be irresponsible and become overwhelmed with concerns that are out of our control.

If we do, what happens to the "concerns" circle? It gets bigger...
and our center circle erodes. Two examples might help illustrate.
In working with people, why do 50-50 relationships (you do your
part; I'll do mine) never work? It's because we're never sure
when the other person has met us half-way. Our tendency is to
selfishly see "our 50%" more than their contribution. When we
focus on the other person, rather than our own behavior, we tend
to see the negative. My personal responsibility in a relationship
(whatever the boundaries) is 100% – not 50%.

In business, if you talk to a successful sales person and ask him to
list the reasons for success, you might hear the following list,
"Well, I get up early; I get on the phone; I don't quit until I get
so-many appointments; I study my presentation; I work out
often..." What's the operative word in those phrases: "I." Ask a
struggling sales person, and the answers are often far different.
You might hear, "It's the lousy economy; our poor product line;
the competition; no supervision from management; little or no
training; the territory was cut..." Where's the focus here?
Somewhere, "out there" is the problem. All – however legitimate
– are out of the sales person's control. And to focus on them
renders the individual stuck in a multitude of excuses.

From now on, we're going to change the words "responsibility"
and "concerns" within the circles of control to... you guessed it...
goals and desires. The inner circle we'll call goals and the outer
circle desires. The reasoning is both simple and crucial: our
responsibilities are good goals; our concerns we desire to change.

Implementing Goals and Desires

So how does it all work? How do we separate goals from desires and make the Serenity Prayer come alive? Here are three key principles that make this truth relevant in everyday circumstances.

Goals:
1.   You <u>work</u> towards them.
2.   They have to do with <u>activities</u>, not outcomes.
3.   They are <u>schedulable</u> and <u>predictable</u>.

Desires:
1.   You <u>pray</u> for them.
2.   They have to do with <u>results</u>.
3.   They are unscheduled, <u>unpredictable</u>, and sometimes serendipitous.

You cannot have a goal to increase your sales by 10%. <u>You</u> can study and learn all there is to learn about your product, your competition, and your customer. <u>You</u> can present the solution that offers the highest quality, the lowest price and the best delivery, but *<u>you</u> cannot force the buyer to give you the purchase order. That decision is out of your hands and control.* Increasing one's sales by 10% is thus a desire... it is out of your control, you can pray for it to happen, and you can be fortunate enough for it to occur.

The attainment of a desire can be assisted by the achievement of a goal. In the example above, your goal might be to learn as much as humanly possible about your product, spend the time and energy to get to know your customer and discover his or her "pain," and to do in-depth research on the competition. In other words, *your goal may be to do your "homework" to the very best of your ability.* And by doing that, you might improve your chances of having the buyer decide in your favor. *But there are no guarantees, because the buyer's decision is completely out of your control.* You may hit the home run or you may strike out, but either way you can feel good about yourself and satisfied because you did your best and gave it your very best effort.

It could be that two thoughts are battling away at this point. First, isn't this just a "semantics" issue, just a different way of defining terms? While it is true that the two words goals/desires are not the issue (call one "X", the other "Y"), the fundamental difference rests in control or lack of it. Secondly, we all have to decide if we are truly helpless in a situation or just haven't seized the need to control it. Laziness, passivity or lack of creativity do not qualify as "I might as well pray about it; it's out of my control." When incentive is high enough, it's amazing how we can suddenly be in control with brilliant creativity!

Time for a pop quiz. Take the following 10 statements and mark each as a goal or desire. The concept is simple enough. Understanding its application is more difficult.

Goals or Desires?	Goal	Desire
To win the League Championship this year.	____	____
To make Chairman's Council (top level) in sales.	____	____
To lose 15 pounds over the next 60 days.	____	____
To make $10,000 over the next two months.	____	____
To shoot 70 over 18 holes of golf.	____	____
(You only have two choices - fantasy is not one of them)		
To communicate better with my daughter.	____	____
To finish that book by the week-end.	____	____
To see a counselor for my stress.	____	____
To work out three times a week.	____	____
To not get angry with my husband.	____	____

(ANSWER: The first five are desires; the last five are goals.)

A New Way to Look at Goals

We work for our goals. The only thing we can control is our own behavior. The achievement of goals is aided immensely by an accountability partner – a friend who will "hold our feet to the fire" through a candid dialogue. Asking the tough questions is not easy to do or to hear, but as the old proverb says, "The kisses of an enemy are treacherous, but the wounds of a friend bring healing." Caring confrontation gets us off the dime.

On the other side of the ledger, the first principle for getting our desires is not independent work, but prayer. Since desires are out of our control, an outside Source is needed. Now we often labor in prayer. While "talking to God" may be short and quick, there are times when "groaning too deep for words" calls for exhausting collaboration. In fact, "desires" must never be thought of as the passive side and "goals" the aggressive side. Both sides require work – <u>patiently</u> waiting for results requires enormous energy. The same often goes for prayer. As the old missionary statesman said, "It's a very busy day. I'll never get it all done. So... before I begin, I'll pray an hour longer."

Goals deal, secondly, with activities. Again, activities we control. If a salesperson wants five appointments for the week, the only thing controllable are the number of telephone dials, not the people agreeing to meet. Even if five say "yes," it's still a desire that they show up, listen, have a need and buy.

That's where the second principle governing desires comes in: Results. We can never become attached to outcomes. Ask the farmer who plants, waters, cultivates and waits, only to see scorching temperatures sear the land and produce zero results. Has the farmer become a sudden failure even though previous years have yielded plenty because of equal hard labor and gentle rains? The true harvest may come at the end of the age, not at the end of the season.

This brings up a key point for mental health. Goals have to do with excellence; desires have to do with success. While we all want to be successful (and stay employed), if "all you can do is your best" (a proper goal attitude) then being internally excellent is enough. How can anybody do more than their best? Have you ever worked for or related to someone you just can't please? No matter what, it's never enough. Mixing up goals and desires will create sleepless nights and potential health problems in dealing with that kind of person. The person with an internal standard of excellence may lose the battle, but always writes the last chapter and wins the war. A boss may fire you. A spouse may reject you. A friend may walk away. But even in the midst of emotional pain, an honest appraisal of excellence versus success will help bring peace or produce change.

The third principle that makes this work is knowing that goals are predictable and can be scheduled. Put them in your pocket calendar and book them. You alone can pull it off, so schedule the goals and get to work on those activities.

A desire, again, is opposite: it is unscheduled and unpredictable. Like an "out of the blue" bit of serendipity, desires often come when we least expect them. For example, the best marketing plan in the world often takes place when I answer my phone and the seeds that I planted months ago and had given up as a lost cause suddenly blossom. Events out of my control have moved the prospect to buy. Ever happened to you? If you're in sales, it happens with regularity. Keeping the "hopper full" is important as the amount of activity will ultimately determine results. Most of the time, the "when" is in question. An amazing dynamic takes place. The divine partnership of "work as if everything depends on me and pray as if everything depends on God" not only frees us of a striving spirit but gives great anticipation, then delight, when we are surprised by serenity. It's called answered prayer.

Another way to differ between goals and desires is seeing what the motivation is. Desire – like the word implies – deals with "wants." Goals deal with the "will." Most of the time we simply call a real desire a goal because we want it so badly. That's fine, but intensity is of little value and may cause great frustration if the object of our desires is dead set against it (has control). We see it all the time in marriages that are failing. One party says, "I'll do anything to get you back," and may set it up as a goal. The other person has thrown in the towel and given up. Understanding goals vs. desires separates the two.

So, in the final analysis, while desires are what we want, goals are what we're willing to do about it. Normally our results are an outgrowth of our discipline (will) and discipline is a result of our passion (wants). I love baseball. My passion for being good at it and seeing strong results (wins, a good batting average, etc.) stirs the discipline necessary to pay the price in goal-setting.

Three Lessons in Life 101

Goals and Desires at Home

Lesson #1: It takes Time:

I vividly remember the first time I brought this new-found fervor to my home and tried it out on the family. I had started to grasp the difference between goals and desires and wanted to share it. As usual, a polite but highly suspect group of four greeted me at the "Family Council" time. Thoughts like, "I wonder what book he's been reading or what tape he's heard" were softly whispered. In characteristic zeal, I unloaded my newly discovered gems! (As a friend of mine said recently, "You know, the older I get, the less I know for sure.") Well, I was sure this was a goldmine of insight. Needless to say, it was met with less than overwhelming enthusiasm. But I pressed on, with pronouncements, examples, definitions, ad nauseam. I even got out the flip chart to illustrate with circles, ledgers and arrows. Being convinced that they had it down pat, we moved into the "workshop" portion of family council, and I got out a bowl and put in each family member's name. We drew names and over the next month, we would hold each other accountable for three goals and pray for each other in three desires. I drew my oldest daughter, Whitney, a junior at the time attending the University of Arkansas. She drew my name, and we began to work on our goals and desires. After my brilliant analysis and teaching prowess, Whitney presented me with the following:

Goal #1. "Dad, I would like for Tom (a recent acquaintance) to like me." Good goal? Certainly a strong desire, but a bit out of her control! I said to Whitney, "Since that's a desire, not a goal, is there anything you alone can do to enter his world, become a more varied and interesting person so he might respond to you?" (Here's a hint. Tom loved baseball. Whitney at the time didn't know the difference between a baseball and an orange.) So what could she alone do? Learn about baseball, buy a ticket and attend a college game with Tom, read the box score and learn the terms. She agreed to learn some vocabulary words. We started with some simple ones: dugout, pitcher's mound, bullpen. Towards the end, we got down deep... balk, sacrifice fly, suicide squeeze, cut-seam fastball. In 21 days, she had learned the words and passed the pop-quiz with flying colors. (She had worked hard, scheduled her activities to memorize the terms and we were praying for results!) About two weeks later she called me, "Dad, guess what! During the 5th inning of one of the games, I saw one of the terms leap off the page. I said, 'Tom, with less than two out and men on first and third, that guy squared around and faced the pitcher as the fella on third ran on the pitch. Why did he put that suicide squeeze down on the third base line rather than the first base line?' After he nearly choked on his drink and swallowed his hot dog whole, Tom said, "Whitney, where have you been all my life?" They then began a conversation they had never had, proving the truth of the statement, "Commitment will hold the relationship together, only communication gives it life."

Here was her second goal: "I'd like to make an 'A' in Spanish this semester." Now on the surface, this sounded like a reasonable "goal." But the more I thought about it, the more I asked the question, "Who's in control here?" The answer (as we have all discovered in school in getting a "C" when we had without question earned an "A") was painfully clear: the teacher! I said to

Whitney, "Why don't we get a tutor, and I'll pay for her services. You study hard after you meet with her once a week, and we'll pray for an 'A'." She agreed to it and she studied like a demon. Guess what she got? You guessed it... a "B"! And guess what she was? Content. At peace with herself. She said it best. "Dad, I discovered a simple truth: all you can do is all you can do."

Her third goal was, "I'd like to stop biting my fingernails by Christmas." Is that a good goal? Certainly. Only Whitney can do that. Only she can read so many books, jog so long, push herself back from the table if she wants to lose weight. Lots of things in her control. Many more things not.

Never become attached to outcomes because they are completely outside of your control. Do, however, learn to be content with having done your best and feel good about the work you did and the effort you put forth. If you place your feeling of success and self-worth into the hands of someone or something outside your control, you are setting yourself up for unnecessary stress, unhappiness and frustration. Understanding goals and desires requires the step of putting things I cannot control into other capable Hands. Otherwise, we're just crossing them off our "goals list" but not removing the churn.

So, one could paraphrase the Serenity Prayer:

God, help me put my efforts into the things that are in my control.
Let me turn over to You the things that are not,
And help me see and understand the difference.

Goals and Desires in Disappointment

<u>Lesson #2: It takes Testing:</u>

Have you ever found yourself bitterly disappointed when a wish failed to come true? When you think back to these disappointments, how many of them were desires which included the actions (or non-actions) of people outside of yourself? I would venture to guess that most of these experiences involved actions that were outside of your individual control.

The path to successfully fulfilling our desires is never a certain one. And diligently as we pursue our goals, we are never guaranteed that we will have the desired outcome. The Serenity Prayer still holds; we have given the situation our best and fallen short, so we move ahead knowing that we must accept things that are beyond our control.

My daughter had just entered high school and was intimidated by the schedule, the work load, the logistics of hauling around a backpack-full of heavy books, and a sea of unfamiliar faces. Within the first eight weeks, she had stumbled in her best subject, English, by forgetting to bring in some assignments she had completed. In her previous classes, she had been able to turn in late assignments and still receive a grade. But now the English teacher refused to give her any credit, and the zero grades had pulled her overall average down to a low "D."

She developed some goal activities to raise her grade, including extra preparation for tests and quizzes, turning in "extra credit" work, and the diligent submission of all assignments in a timely manner. In spite of this activity, she was not able to raise her grade above a "C," the lowest semester grade she had ever made. She came home with her report card clinched in her hand and her eyes red from weeping.

"I can't believe I made a 'C.' I set my goals and I worked hard, but it didn't make any difference!"

As we discussed her frustration, I asked her if she had done all she possibly could to raise her grade. She said she had. So I asked if she felt more peace of mind from knowing that she had given it her best effort versus not applying her maximum energy to the situation.

"But it didn't make any difference!" she replied disappointedly.

No, it didn't this time, I agreed. And there would be plenty of other times when her best efforts would fall short. But she would always know that she had given it her best. And more than likely, her teacher would know this as well.

It took several weeks for her to get beyond the anger she was feeling, but she finally did. And for the rest of that academic year, she made "A's" in English and never had any difficulty getting her assignments in on a timely basis. The lack of immediate results paved the way for a long-term change in behavior and attitude.

Goals and Desires in the Workplace

Lesson #3: It takes Tenacity:

Bill was an outstanding young life insurance agent for New York Life. Although he had less than a year of experience, he was already competing for success in a sales contest. With less than a week to go, he needed one more major sale to assure him of victory and a fully paid vacation to Hawaii.

The timing could not have been better. He was working on a large case with Jerry, the owner of a small, rapidly growing computer services company. Bill had met Jerry through a mutual friend at church, and they had already met three times to review all of Jerry's needs. Bill had put together an illustration which he believed would best serve Jerry, and he had scheduled a final meeting which would most certainly end with a close. The sale of this universal life policy would also assure him of success in the sales contest. His wife had already begun to make plans for the vacation in Maui.

But the day before the meeting he received a phone call from Jerry.

"Bill, you won't believe this, but I just received a call from my best friend and fraternity brother from college. He's gone into the insurance business, and as you can imagine, I promised to work with him on my policy. I'm sorry to do this after all the time you spent working with me, but I'm sure you can understand."

Bill stumbled through a quick good-bye and then sat, stunned, pondering his fate. It was certainly not the first time this type of situation had occurred, but it came at a particularly devastating time for Bill. He immediately told his wife and let the bad news begin to sink in.

But the next day, after a long, sleepless night, Bill returned to the situation with new resolve and a different direction. He called Jerry to enroll him in a new idea.

"Jerry, I just wanted to call and thank you for being honest with me about your obligation to your friend, and I just want you to know that I completely respect and honor your decision. I'm not calling to try to change your mind, but I did have another idea. Has your company initiated a 401K plan yet?"

Jerry paused. "Why, no, we haven't."

"Given what you've shared with me about where your company is right now, I believe it would be an advantageous time to look at this opportunity for you and your employees. Would you be open to giving me another chance to work with you?"

"Certainly, Bill. Come on out tomorrow."

The upshot was that Bill didn't make the trip to Hawaii, his first desire. But his persistent goal activities paid off, and Jerry's company became one of his best clients.

Bill got it...not every desire is attainable, no matter how outstanding our goal activity is, because desires involve actions and commitments from people outside of our control. If we really believe this and work through our goals, we will enjoy the best of mental and emotional health as well as experiencing business prosperity.

But most of us stumble along the way. We allow frustrations to derail our activity. Anger and bitterness hijack our hearts, and we fall short of applying the truths of the Serenity Prayer to our lives.

What happens and how can we change? How can we use goals and desires to live life on purpose? If knowledge allows you to take things apart and wisdom helps you put things back together, how can we apply this knowledge in a wise way?

Strategies to Make it Happen

It was 1653, a time of civil war and social upheaval in England. Oliver Cromwell had become head of state, and one day he condemned a young soldier to death. He was scheduled to die at the ringing of the curfew bell. The soldier was engaged to a young woman who came to Cromwell and begged passionately for the Lord Protector to spare her betrothed's life. But Cromwell showed no mercy, and the town awaited the execution at the tolling of the bell. At the appointed hour, the executioner solemnly entered the tower and pulled repeatedly on the ancient rope, but no sound emerged.

The soldier's sweetheart had ascended to the top of the belfry, reached out and caught hold of the huge tongue of the bell. And as the rope was being pulled, she held on while being smashed against the sides of the iron bell. At length, the bell ceased to swing. She fell to the ground and struggled into Cromwell's sight to beseech him once more for mercy on the life of her true love. A poet standing in the crowd captured the event with these lines:

"At his feet she told her story,
showed her hands all bruised and torn
And her sweet young face,
still haggard with the anguish it had worn
Touched his heart with sudden pity,
lit his eyes with misty light,
"Go!" said Cromwell, "Your lover lives!
Curfew will not sing tonight."

It would be wonderful if all our goal-directed efforts led to such immediate and heroic victories. We are inspired by tales of efforts in a harsh, unforgiving world, and part of our human nature is the hope that impels us to dream the dream of success against all odds. We flock to buy lottery tickets each week even though our odds of winning are slightly worse than being hit by lightening. We are all champions of the underdog because each of us has felt the fear and loneliness that David felt stepping into the arena with Goliath.

Yet the daily grind of our lives reinforces the sense that heroic acts seem few and far between, reserved only for those lucky souls who stumble into the web of fate and destiny where a simple act of courage is illuminated by the floodlights of history. It seems woven into our psychic vision to view life as an inexorable reality punctuated by an occasional great achievement. And in this manner of thinking, we begin to overlook the power of holding tenaciously to the activities that only we can control. We forget the simple power that comes from setting up attainable goals which open us up to the possibility of major achievements. The dream deferred can become the fulfilled desire, the fruit of our disciplined efforts.

In the struggle to marshal our impulses in service of reaching our goals, the war must be waged on three battlefronts – Mind, Emotion, and Will.

The mind is the first challenge. In setting your goals, you must think clearly about your priorities and about what is truly within your control. You should commit your thoughts to paper and hold yourself accountable.

Emotions are the next challenge. They can sabotage the finest plans the mind ever constructed. They can also carry you to the finish line when all else fails. The question is how does one enlist the emotions as a friend, not a foe.

Finally, there is the element of will. Willpower provides the fuel to harness mind and emotions. Will is the spiritual toughness to carry out your goals. Will is the umbilical cord to your dreams.

The following nine strategies arise from Mind, Emotion, and Will. These strategies will help you develop and take ownership of a plan to attain your goals.

MIND
Remembering the Difference

Confusing the difference between goals and desires leads to anxiety in all its myriad forms.

Thoughts determine emotions. Clear thinking leads to feeling deeply and acting consistently. The battle begins in the mind. Confusing the difference between goals and desires leads to anxiety in all its myriad forms. It is not hyperbole to believe that much of the dissatisfaction which plagues modern society derives from the dilemma of understanding what is and isn't under our control. Without this understanding, how can we begin to maximize our goal-directed efforts to better ourselves and reach our desires?

One need only look around to try and find anyone who appears to have a fundamentally consistent working grasp of the Serenity Prayer. How many do you know who fit this category? I know very few.

Yes, there will always be tension between our goals and our desires. It's what we do with this tension that reflects on the strength of our character. Without strength of character, it is highly unlikely that we will reach our desire.

Goals are activities that we create to support the possibility of reaching our desires. Goals are activities that only we can control: how much food we will eat, how many hours a day we will devote to sales calls, how much quality time we will carve out for our family, how much energy we will devote to a specific project.

If the goal depends on someone or something outside of <u>you</u>, it's not a goal. It's a desire. For our desires, pray. It's as much an activity as setting and working goals. People remember very little and change slowly if at all. There is a connection! Goals Vs. Desires: Remember the Difference.

MIND
Finding Balance

**Set goals that will challenge you without being so
unrealistically high that they discourage you.**

One of the most difficult aspects of goal-setting is finding the
right balance. You want to set goals that will challenge you and
vault you out of your comfort zone. On the other hand, goals that
are unrealistically high will have the effect of discouraging you
and eroding confidence. The line between these two can be very
thin.

The toughest decision that many of us face on a consistent basis
is to know whether to let go or to hang on. This has been true for
me because there is always a group of folks whispering in one
ear, "Keep the faith! Where is your perseverance? Stay the
course! Never, never give up!"

And that sounds pretty good. Then there is another group that
whispers, "Where is your wisdom! Let go. You have been
admirably tenacious, but the horse is dead. Get off the horse."

These two voices whisper in my ear all of the time. Do I let go of
this? Do I hang on to that? Did I do enough here? Should I have
done more of that?

This dilemma revolves around the painstaking task of setting your
goals at the right level. Here are two considerations. First, your
goals should be sufficiently high to nudge you out of you comfy
box. The way to tell is to see if a sacrifice has been made. What

did I give up? A friend of mine recently gave up watching Monday Night Football to instead help his son with homework and organize the upcoming week at school. He says the results have been dramatic.

The second consideration is that you shouldn't set unrealistically high, unattainable goal activities. To aspire to lose 20 pounds is completely realistic and attainable. But to expect to lose 20 pounds in one week is to invite failure, not to mention potential health hazards.

If you are vexed about any of your goal setting, seek outside counsel. There is a wonderful custom in the Quaker community called the "clearness committee." In essence, you would invite a half dozen trusted friends to help discern the value and direction of your goals. In this process, the group refrains from giving you advice but spends three hours asking you honest, open questions to help you discover your own internal guidance system.

I have been truly blessed in my life to have had mentors guide me along my chosen path. Some of the best counsel they have given has not been in the form of advice but in the form of simple questions. "What would you like most about achieving this goal? How would you deal with certain setbacks?"

To stay on track, create your own "clearness committee."

MIND
The Inevitable Tension

Realize there will always be tension between goals and desires, and use this tension to further your growth.

When desires are not reached, use this as an opportunity to learn and grow.

The measure of a man is how he deals with adversity. Delight in the possibility of growing stronger when failure occurs.

While in the ministry a number of years, I learned the wisdom of the statement, "A leader is one with the head of a scholar, the heart of a child and the skin of a rhino. The problem is that the heart and skin often change places." I would prepare messages, counsel people in trouble, lead tired board members and struggle with seeing little change. I rationalized, "Why work so hard when so little is achieved?" Becoming increasingly hardened and cynical about people and progress, I flirted with burn-out and suffered bursts of anger. My problem in hindsight was assuming responsibility (control) I was never intended to have. I was assuming responsibility for people/circumstances rather than being responsive to them. In essence, I got goals and desires out of kilter and the inevitable tension became an albatross.

Don't dwell on the negative. It will rob the joy. Life's tension is that it's a mystery to be lived, not a puzzle to be fixed.

EMOTIONS
The Stealthy Hijackers

Don't allow your emotions to derail goal-directed activities.

They are as nasty and sinister a gang as ever hijacked an airplane or held a group hostage. You know this gang well... they're the emotions constantly roiling around inside you. Anger, anxiety, resentment, frustration... these feelings are the stealthy hijackers of our goals and desires.

Is it possible to keep this gang under control? How do we do this?

Much has been written about "emotional intelligence," and this is the key essence: those who know how to marshal their impulses in service of a higher goal THRIVE. Those who are unable to control their emotions FAIL.

Does this mean we are not meant to feel pain and anguish? Certainly not. These are necessary, everyday aspects of being human. They come with the territory, and are in fact more responsible for human growth than anything else. But how do we prevent this gang from hijacking the airplane of our life?

Dr. Victor Frankl was an Austrian psychiatrist who was captured by the Nazis during World War II and sent to Auschwitz concentration camp. His wife and parents had been murdered by the SS, and he experienced the most horrible atrocities imaginable. Enduring hunger, filth, torture, and lack of sleep, he came upon a powerful discovery. He realized that the Nazis could control virtually every aspect of his life except one factor: they could not dictate to him how he would react to and process his treatment.

Only he could control this. In order to keep his sanity, he realized he would have to endure this excruciating time and somehow find a sense of purpose to fortify his mind and heart. He developed the following guideline to live by: "We only know and experience this life through the meaning or the relevance of the perceptions that we assign to it."

Dr. Frankl used this knowledge to survive. He overcame his suffering through his commitment and ability to marshal his impulses in service of a loftier desire. From his experiences, he wrote the inspiring book, Man's Search for Meaning. The truth that emerges from this book is simple yet profound: we are in charge of how we perceive and react to every situation we encounter in life. We can give the emotional hijackers the keys to our plane. Or we can keep the gang of emotions under control as we stay on track with our goals.

It's your choice.

EMOTIONS
The Passion Dance

Pursue your goals with enthusiasm, passion, and authenticity.

"Ever since there have been men, man has given himself over to
too little joy. That, my brothers, is our original sin. I should
believe only in a God who understood how to dance."

- Henri Matisse

All of these strategies we have explored will fail if they're not
pursued with enthusiasm and fervor. When you believe you have
few resources remaining, passion will carry you through.
Without enthusiasm, you are no more than a robot going through
the motions.

If you haven't tapped into your passion, you should listen to the
inner voice calling to you. This is the voice God has given you to
fulfill the original selfhood He gave you at birth.

We spend a great deal of our lives running away from this
package of God-given gifts that make up our unique self. Martin
Buber recounts a Hasidic tale that reveals the tendency for each
of us to desire to be someone else and the fundamental
importance of becoming one's self. Rabbi Zusya, when he was
an old man, said, "In the coming world, they will not ask me:
'why were you not Moses?' They will ask me: 'why were you
not Zusya?'"

Find your gifts and talents, and be true to them. Honor your strengths, and they will carry you far.

As Duke Ellington once said, "It don't mean a thing if it ain't got that swing."

Send the robot home and hit the dance floor. You can let joy be the light that leads you through every day.

EMOTIONS
Nurture Your Temple

Poor health will drain your emotional strength. Take care of yourself.

To effectively reach our goals, we must be in optimum physical and intellectual condition. Remember that the "holy trinity" of good health - proper nutrition, consistent exercise, and sufficient rest - will help you deal with the stress and anxiety that will invariably cross your path. Feed and nurture <u>yourself</u>!

A friend of mine recently was going through a turbulent time. In one month, he had been laid off his job of 20 years in a corporate downsizing, struggled with a situation in which his son was suspended from school for disciplinary problems, and, not surprisingly, he had developed severe stomach pains. He wondered aloud if perhaps he was experiencing his first ulcer.

I asked him if he had been to see a doctor.

He laughed and said that the stomach was the least of his problems. He would create a resume, talk to some search firms, and set up a time to visit the headmaster at his son's school. The stomach problems would have to wait.

After a lengthy discussion, I finally convinced him to tackle his own physical problems first. Without the confidence of a healthy engine, he would be flailing around like a car out of control on an icy road. Grudgingly, he made an appointment that day to see a gastroenterologist.

Why is it that we have such a difficult time taking care of our own health issues first? In my friend's case, he admitted later to being a "clutcher." Clutchers manage anxiety by seeking more intimacy in a relationship. In his situation, he dealt with his anxiety by leaning on his wife and children. While the desire for intimacy is normally a healthy one, it becomes unhealthy when it masks your inability to tenaciously pursue your goals. When we fail to stay within the discipline we intended, we seek the consolation of a loved one.

And "consolation" is what we get: the consolation prize! Nice try, you gave it your best, you got halfway there, now snuggle up and we'll forget the rest of it together.

Stay focused on the things that will make you successful in attaining your goals... your skills, your physical energy, your positive attitude. As part of setting your goals, you should always include activities targeted to improve your health, elevate your skills, stimulate your mind, and expand your talents.

It's all about giving yourself the fuel you need to get where you're going. Make sure you keep your tank full.

WILL
Put It in Writing

Express your goals positively and precisely in writing.

Express your goals positively and precisely in writing. Putting goals in writing will force you to give sufficient thought to what you are doing and how you will go about doing it. It avoids confusion and gives force to your intentions.

To say that, "I will take the time necessary to contact 20 clients for face-to-face appointments this week," is really a desire and not a goal, since it involves the decisions and commitments of someone outside of yourself. Expressed as a goal, this might look more like, "I will spend four hours on Monday and four hours on Tuesday contacting clients to arrange as many as 20 face-to-face appointments for Wednesday, Thursday, and Friday of this week."

Be careful about expressing goals negatively. "I will avoid making the mistake of closing too hard and alienating potential new clients," is not as effective as, "I will use all of my empathic listening skills to insure that all my sales calls this week are effective and productive."

It's time to put this theory into practice. In the following pages, we have provided you with the scaffolding on which to build your goals and desires. Now it is up to you. Put your goals in writing, set them adequately high, place a time deadline on your activities, and work your plan!

We have divided this blueprint into three areas: personal development, relationships, and work. We suggest you start with three desires and three goals for each domain using a simple, one-page worksheet. Before starting, try to follow these seven tips:

1) Start With the Desires First

Begin with the "want to" side. It's always easier to imagine what you want to have rather than what you need to do.

2) Visualize the Desires Completed

Seeing your desires already accomplished not only exercises faith, but paints a sharper image on the mind of what it will look like.

3) Limit the Time Frame to 90 Days

Rather than getting bogged down on long-term goals and desires, we respond better with quicker affirmation that we're on track. Feedback is faster.

4) Get an Accountability Partner

A friend who will pray for us in the desires department and "hold our feet to the fire" in the goals area is critical. A partner will also help clarify whether the goals and desires are defined correctly.

5) Limit the Number of Goals and Desires

Start with only one goal and one desire in the personal development area. Then move to the relationship domain. Resist the temptation to list several under each area. One goal accomplished will effect other unwritten goals, while too many listed diffuses our focus. Expand each area only after the initial 90 days.

5) *Teach Others Only After Three Months of Trial and Error*

Without the experience of working this approach for at least a quarter, any sharing with others lacks authenticity. It will come across like a book report – nice concept but without heart.

6) *Use the Worksheet First on Your Family or Friends*

When sharing the concept, use it with one family member or friend who is struggling with a problem "out of their control." Goals-and-Desires come alive in a counseling context.

"Life is like three ships. They must be seaworthy (personal development); they must not run into each other (relationships); and they must know which direction they are headed (calling/work)."

-C. S. Lewis

A Sample Worksheet

Goals	Desires
Personal Development	**Personal Development**
Workout 3 times a week at gym - M, W, F at 8 p.m. OR Read my Bible and pray for 20 minutes every morning.	Lose 15 lbs. In the next 90 days OR Grow Spiritually
Relationships Listen to a tape on time management; ask Beth for a "date" once a week for 15 minutes; count to 10 before reacting/exploding OR Call Bill and continue until I reach him (no time limit)	**Relationships** Better communication with my daughter – we talk to each other pleasantly. OR Re-commit to my estranged brother.
Work Call new prospects for 1 hour every morning (8-9 a.m.) before making calls in the field.	**Work** Make $15,000 in new commissions over next 90 days.
Get to work by 7 a.m. every day and home by 6:30 p.m.	Make Million Dollar Round Table

Goals	Desires
Personal Development	Personal Development
Relationships	Relationships
Work	Work

WILL
Accountability

Keep your goals measurable and achievable.

You are looking for motivation and accountability. If you base your goals on personal performance targets, you can maintain control over them and derive inspiration from their completion. But if you set up your goals based upon outcomes that involve other people or outside sources, you have initiated a desire, not a goal.

In 1953, Ben Hogan achieved something that no one before or after has been able to do. It is an accomplishment that many still look upon as not only the greatest golfing feat of all time, but as one of the greatest accomplishments in sporting history. After recovering from a major automobile accident in which doctors believed he would never walk again, Hogan returned to the game to do what some considered impossible. He entered only seven tournaments and won five of them. He entered three of the majors (the U.S. Open, the Masters, and the British Open) and won all three of them, a feat no one has ever accomplished. He did not enter the PGA Championship that year since it required that players walk 36 holes a day as part of its match play format, and he did not believe his legs were capable of withstanding that endurance test.

When a sportswriter interviewed Hogan about his feat, he asked him, "What was your goal as you set about preparing for this season?" Hogan replied, "To be 100% focused on each shot of every round I played." The interviewer appeared not to have heard Hogan's very specific response, and he asked again, "Did you believe that you could win three majors?" Without batting a steely eye, Hogan once again responded, "You asked me what my goal was, and it was to be 100% focused on every shot of every competitive round I played."

Ben Hogan understood the difference between goals and desires, and that understanding undoubtedly led to his enormous success. With each shot he faced, he did not have an image of a shining trophy being handed to him, not did he hear the applause of thousands as his final putt disappeared in the cup. He was completely focused on the lie of the ball, the distance to the flag, the factoring of the wind and the elevation, and exactly what kind of shot he wanted to play. And as he took the club back, his concentration was absolute. Nothing would enter his mind to prevent him from making the best possible swing he could.

Those who were close to Hogan knew that besides being one of the fiercest competitors the game had ever known, he was also one of its most indefatigable workers. He would practice for hours attempting to master on a particular shot. Fellow members at Shady Oaks Country Club in Fort Worth used to watch Ben hit hundreds of balls with just one club - a five-iron - in his tireless pursuit of perfection. Even while practicing, he showed a keen grasp of the critical difference between goals and desires. And when he teed off the first hole of every new tournament, he did so with the confidence that he could not have practiced and prepared more diligently. The desires would take care of themselves... and so they did.

While we often think of legendary athletic feats as the act of a singular will - Babe Ruth pointing his bat toward the outfield bleachers predicting a home run - the reality is much closer to the path which Ben Hogan took. Years of practice and following small, measurable goals lead to incrementally higher skill and performance levels, which in turn lead to the attainment of championships and victory. Is a certain amount of innate, God-given talent necessary? Absolutely. But what is it that separates the very good from the great? It is the tenacity with which one practices and pursues his goals. This is the real preparation for attainment of desires.

WILL
To Serve is to Win

Explore all your opportunities to serve others.

"He who will live for others shall have great troubles, but they shall seem to him small.
He who will live for himself shall have small troubles, but they shall seem to him great."

    - William R. Inge

As you explore your desires, look at the circles of influence you are touching. Who are you helping? Who are you serving?

One of the great rewards of pursuing your goal activities in a disciplined, enthusiastic way is the beneficial fallout to all those around you. Your spouse, your family, your friends, your company, your church... all will gladly soak up the grace of your positive efforts.

There is an old business model that declares nice guys finish last, only the shark survives, and so on. It's corporate Darwinianism, and thankfully, it's an endangered species that is disappearing faster than a polyester leisure suit.

In its place is a new, robust paradigm that looks first to serve others. From this model emerges "the customer is always right" and counselor-selling styles. Empathy is the key ingredient, and service is the goal.

Here are some questions to consider:

1. Who are you serving and how can you expand the circle of those your activities touch?
2. Do your business activities help your company grow and prosper?
3. Are your business activities directly aligned with the goals of the company?
4. Do your desires create a WIN-WIN scenario for all those you love?
5. How are you making a difference in the lives of those around you?

Moving Forward

So what's the payoff, you ask, for the disciplined striving toward goals within our control?

Most of us labor in the shadowlands, that lonely place between victory and defeat. We settle for mediocrity. We do just enough to get by. And we wake up one day to see that we have lived our lives as spectators.

Life rewards <u>activity</u>, not ungrounded intention. Goals vs. desires is more than a token "good idea" or a new way to list things. A new approach to "packaging" will simply not solve the problem.

Life rewards the relentless pursuit of goals. Without that pursuit, the outer circle of desires will remain a distant dream.

Be clear about your goals. Assemble a "clearness committee" to keep you on track.

You are wired for wonder, not for worry -- or fear and guilt. It's your choice.

Embrace the Serenity Prayer. Live it and pray it.

What Canvas Awaits

He wakes up in the middle of the night at the sound of his wife's soft breathing. He thinks about what awaits him today, and he is filled with a sense of optimism and hope. As he begins to plot out his day at work, he realizes that he has started to predict and plan for events and circumstances that are out of his control. He catches himself and prays the prayer which has now become a radar guidance system for his soul:

> "God, grant me the Serenity
> To accept the thing I cannot change;
> Courage to change the things I can;
> And Wisdom to know the difference."

He smiles and senses himself filled with an inner satisfaction that has eluded him until recently. Where these early mornings had once created a sense of dread, he now senses the miracle of his many blessings.

> "Living one day at a time;
> Enjoying one moment at a time."

He turns to admire his wife, still sailing along in slumber. Looking at her face, he sees the journey they have experienced together, with all of its anguish and wonder. And in this brief moment, he is exceedingly thankful for what a strong partner she has been.

> "Accepting hardship as the pathway to peace
> Taking, as He did, this sinful world as it is

Not as I would have it."

And all of the problems at work suddenly begin to array themselves as opportunities for growth. He sees that he has wasted too many hours planning for what he cannot control, worrying over matters that only God can resolve.

"Trusting that He will make all things right
If I surrender to His will."

He bundles together these looming problems and offers them up to God, his arms extended and his palms up in a gesture of supplication. As he stretches, he feels a weight removed from his heart. In its place is a lightness that defies anxiety.

"That I may be reasonably happy in this life
And supremely happy with Him forever in the next."

The day begins to dawn, and he feels a wondrous grace. A new painting to behold.

"Dad, I need you to get me to school early this morning!"

The telephone rings. Someone at work needs him to return the call. His wife is asking him about plans. As he scurries to his car, he laughs at the morning chaos and celebrates all the challenges he will face today.

And miraculously, framed against the eastern horizon, the colors spread slowly across the fresh canvas.

If you are interested in purchasing additional copies of this book, please contact us at:

Alliance Affinity Group, L.L.C.
9559 Atherton Drive
Dallas, TX 75243
1-888-692-6114

email: randy.zack@worldnet.att.net